08 JUN 2022   WITHDRAWN

ROBERT SCOTT IN THE ANTARCTIC

Philip Sauvain

A ZOË BOOK

A ZOË BOOK

© 1993 Zoë Books Limited

Devised and produced by
Zoë Books Limited
15 Worthy Lane
Winchester
Hampshire SO23 7AB
England

First published in Great Britain in 1993 by
Zoë Books Limited
15 Worthy Lane
Winchester
Hampshire SO23 7AB

A CIP catalogue record for this book is available from the British Library.

ISBN 1 874488 28 2

Printed in Italy by Grafedit SpA
Design: Jan Sterling, Sterling Associates
Picture research: Faith Perkins
Maps: Gecko Limited
Production: Grahame Griffiths

Photographic acknowledgements

The publishers wish to acknowledge, with thanks, the following photographic sources:

Aspect Picture Library: 11b, 18b; The British Library: 19, 28t; The Cavalry and Guards Club: 27; Robert Harding Picture Library: 23 (© Roald Amundsen Museum); Michael Holford 6, 7t; Mountain Camera/Colin Monteath: title, 5, 28b; Popperfoto: 4b, 13b, 15t, 16t, 16b, 17, 20, 21t, 22t, 22b, 24t, 24b, 25; The Royal Geographical Society: 8, 9t (National Antarctic Expedition), 13t, 18t (Ponting), 29 (Roger Mear); Science Photograph Library 7b (Doug Allan); Scott Polar Research Institute: 10, 11t, 12, 14, 15b (Ponting), 21b (Ponting), 26b

Cover photographs courtesy of Mountain Camera/Colin Monteath and Popperfoto

Contents

Death in the snow

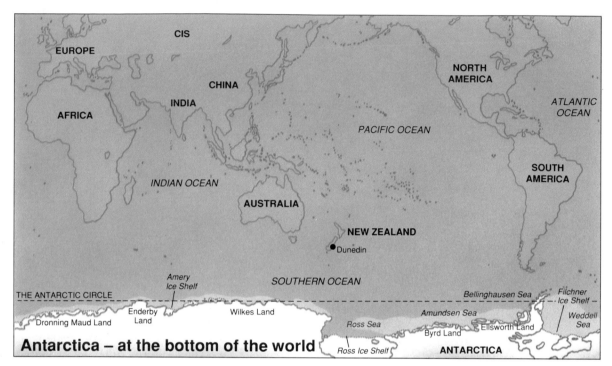

EUROPE

CIS

CHINA

INDIA

AFRICA

INDIAN OCEAN

PACIFIC OCEAN

NORTH AMERICA

ATLANTIC OCEAN

SOUTH AMERICA

AUSTRALIA

NEW ZEALAND

•Dunedin

Amery Ice Shelf

SOUTHERN OCEAN

Bellinghausen Sea

Filchner Ice Shelf

THE ANTARCTIC CIRCLE

Enderby Land

Wilkes Land

Dronning Maud Land

Amundsen Sea

Weddell Sea

Ross Sea

Byrd Land

Ellsworth Land

Antarctica – at the bottom of the world

Ross Ice Shelf

ANTARCTICA

In March 1912 exciting news reached Oslo, the capital of Norway. The Norwegian explorer, Roald Amundsen, had reached the South Pole, the most southerly point on the surface of the Earth, in the **continent** of Antarctica. However the same news alarmed many people in Britain. A British explorer, Captain Robert Falcon Scott, had gone to Antarctica at the same time as Amundsen, and yet there was no news of him. Where was Scott? What had happened to the members of his team? Did they reach the South Pole before or after Amundsen? Indeed, were they still alive?

Questions of life and death

At Scott's Antarctic **base camp**, on McMurdo Sound, the other members of

▼ Roald Amundsen was the first to reach the South Pole.

▲ The worried British expedition members were waiting at Scott's base camp.

the British expedition also waited anxiously for news of their friends. It was now nearly April which is the beginning of the Antarctic winter.

Some of the team had already given up hope. They knew Scott and his team could not hope to last through the winter without extra food and supplies such as fuel for their cooking stoves. At that time there were no portable **wireless sets**. The team had no means of keeping in touch with Scott. Nor did they have telephone or radio links with Britain. A leading member of his team, called Apsley Cherry-Garrard, made a note in his diary: 'We have got to face it now. The **Pole Party** will not in all probability ever get back. And there is no more we can do.'

In search of Scott

On 12 November 1912 Cherry-Garrard and a search party found Scott's tent. It was only 18 km (11 miles) from a large storage **depot** which they had all helped to stock with food and oil over a year earlier. These stores alone would have been enough for the team to return to the base camp on the coast.

Inside the tent, however, they found the frozen bodies of 'Bill' Wilson, Henry Bowers and Captain Scott himself. Why had they died so close to the food depot? And why were there only three bodies? Captain Lawrence Oates and Petty-Officer Edgar Evans had also been in the Pole Party.

They found the answers to these questions in Captain Scott's **journal**. This was an account of the expedition. Each day, Scott had written down the events of the previous 24 hours. He had noted down how far the team had travelled and their present position. He had also described the weather conditions. In this way the outside world learned what had happened to Scott and his team.

Members of the search party built a **cairn** to mark the spot. They used blocks of ice instead of stones. They had already **cabled** their sad news home, in February 1913. People all over Britain were horrified.

Scott's team may not have been first to the South Pole, and they had lost their lives. However when people learned how they had died, the explorers became heroes.

Exploring Antarctica

Captain Scott and the members of his expedition had been fascinated by Antarctica for years. They knew that it is the only continent without people. Few plants grow there, and there are even fewer animals. Only around the coast are there seals, whales, ocean birds and the comical, flightless penguins.

A world of ice

Unlike the Arctic, the Antarctic is made up of land as well as snow and ice. Its area is half as big again as the United States, twice the size of Australia and 60 times bigger than Britain. It is covered by a great **ice sheet** which is up to 4780 metres (3 miles) thick in places. If all this ice melted, the sea level around the world would rise by about 45 to 60 metres (150-200 feet).

The ice sheet looks completely still, but some of it moves very, very slowly towards the coast. It slides over the land. Where the weather is warm enough to make it melt, large blocks break off to form **icebergs**.

The climate in Antarctica is the most severe in the world. We know this because modern scientists have built **research stations** there. They have now taken

▼ Captain Cook's ships, the *Resolution* and the *Discovery*, sailed past huge icebergs, but Cook did not see any land.

▲ Captain Ross's ships, *Erebus* and *Terror*

accurate weather records for many years. The world's coldest temperature, minus 89.2°C (minus 128.6°F), was recorded at the Vostok research station in 1983. To make matters worse for explorers, winds often blow across Antarctica at **gale force** speeds. They pick up snow and ice, and cause terrible **blizzards** in both winter and summer. People caught in such a storm cannot see, let alone survive the cold.

The unknown land

People had talked about a great land somewhere in the southern oceans for hundreds of years. It was sometimes referred to by a Latin name, *Terra Australis* ('land of the south'). About 200 years ago the English explorer Captain James Cook criss-crossed the oceans in search of this southern continent. His ships sailed in Antarctic waters, but Cook sighted no land.

Fifty years later, seamen hunting seals in the southern oceans did make a number of important discoveries. In 1823

a British **navigator** called Captain James Weddell discovered the sea that now bears his name. In 1838-40 an American naval lieutenant called Charles Wilkes led an expedition to Antarctic waters. He sighted land, which he correctly described as a continent. He was followed in 1839-43 by a British expedition led by Captain James Ross. Ross discovered a great **ice shelf**, a thick sheet of ice which meets the sea as a series of cliffs.

In the 1890s, scientists and explorers began to take an interest in Antarctica once again. An Australian expedition set out for Antarctica in 1894. On another expedition in 1897-99, a ship called the *Belgica* was **marooned** for a whole year in the Antarctic ice. A leading member of its crew was a Norwegian sailor called Roald Amundsen.

A year later a British expedition was organised. The man chosen to lead it was a naval commander called Robert Falcon Scott.

▼ When ice caves like this one on the Ross Ice Shelf collapse, pieces of the shelf may break off to form icebergs.

Scott's first journey

The National Antarctic Expedition of 1901-04 was organised by Britain's Royal Geographical Society, with the help of its president, Sir Clements Markham, and other British scientists. Over £90 000 was raised to pay for the expedition. Half of this sum came from the British government.

Scott's first move was to seek the advice of a great Norwegian explorer called Fridtjof Nansen. Nansen had explored the Arctic Ocean in his ship, the *Fram*. Like Nansen, Scott had a ship specially built for the voyage.

A ship for the ice

Scott's ship was called the *Discovery*. It was only 52 metres (172 feet) long and was very different from most other ships being built at the time. It had no thin iron or steel plates, but extra-thick wooden planking. Scott believed that the thickness of the wood would help to stop icebergs tearing a hole in the sides of the ship. While many new ships in 1900 had coal-burning steam engines, Scott's *Discovery* could also be used as a sailing vessel when wind conditions were right. The reason for this was very simple. Coal was heavy and bulky to carry. There would not be enough room for all the stores and equipment needed for the expedition if they were going to rely entirely on steam power.

To the ends of the earth

Scott and the members of his first expedition left London in August 1901.

They spent two long winters in Antarctica, carrying out useful scientific work. They drew maps of the region. They collected **specimens** and made written records of the things they could see and study. They built a hut in McMurdo Sound, on a part of the coast that Scott called Hut Point.

The most exciting part of the expedition came when Scott led a party of three men southwards over the ice. Their

▼ Scott's ship, the *Discovery*

▲ Hut Point was Scott's first Antarctic base.
The *Discovery* lies offshore.

aim was to get as close as possible to the
South Pole. Scott's two companions were
Ernest Shackleton and Dr Edward Wilson,
who was nicknamed 'Bill'. They reached
82° South. This was the farthest south
anyone had ever been. To get there, they
travelled about 600 km (350 miles) across
the Ross Ice Shelf, a region also known as
the Great Ice Barrier. However mountains
blocked the way to the high land, or

plateau beyond. The South Pole is situated
in this high, flat region, at 2992 metres
(9816 feet) above sea-level.

Dogs and sledges

On the return journey the **huskies** that
they had taken with them began to
weaken. These dogs pulled the sledges
which were loaded with food, a tent and
other equipment. One by one they died,
or had to be killed when they became too
weak to pull the sledges.

In the end, the men were left without
huskies and had to pull the sledges over
the ice themselves. This was unfortunate,
for it made Scott believe that sledges
pulled by huskies were not a reliable form
of transport in the Antarctic.

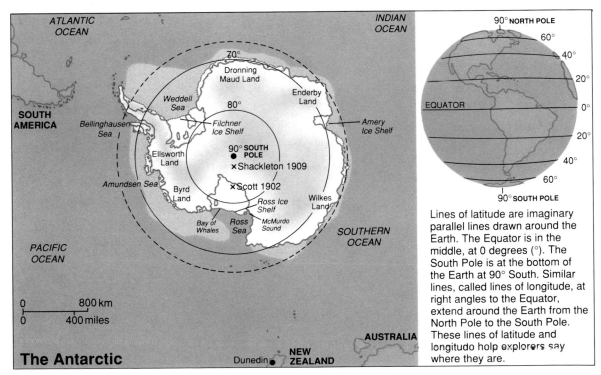

Lines of latitude are imaginary
parallel lines drawn around the
Earth. The Equator is in the
middle, at 0 degrees (°). The
South Pole is at the bottom of
the Earth at 90° South. Similar
lines, called lines of longitude, at
right angles to the Equator,
extend around the Earth from the
North Pole to the South Pole.
These lines of latitude and
longitude help explorers say
where they are.

Scott and Shackleton

The expedition of 1901-04 was a great success. When Scott returned to London he became one of the most famous people in Britain. Rich people asked him to their parties and dances. He was often asked to speak at dinners and other important events. Scott, a shy man, did not like this. He told a friend: 'I've had enough of fame to last me a lifetime. There has been no peace, no quiet – nothing but one mad rush.'

A brave leader

Robert Falcon Scott had been born on 6 June 1868, in the British port of Plymouth, an important naval base. Scott joined the Royal Navy in 1882 and by 1900 he had reached the rank of Commander. The first Antarctic expedition had proved that Scott was a brave and determined leader. Even though he was not a strong man, he had worked as hard as the men under his command. He was promoted to Captain on his return in 1904.

Lieutenant (later Admiral) Edward Evans knew Scott well. He was one of the last people to see Scott alive in 1912. He wrote that Scott was 'a brilliant naval officer' with 'the keen brain of a first class scientist.' 'Looking back over 40 years,' he said in 1943, 'I would class him as one of the three cleverest men I have ever met.'

The Shackleton expedition

Although Scott said that he did not like being famous, he was often very jealous of other people's success. He was annoyed in

▲ Robert Falcon Scott in naval uniform

1907 when his former team-mate Ernest Shackleton began to raise money for a new Antarctic expedition. Scott probably felt that he himself was the obvious choice for leader of a new British expedition. Perhaps that was why he made Shackleton promise not to use the old base camp at Hut Point.

Shackleton reached Antarctica in January 1908, but was unable to keep his promise. He could not find anywhere else suitable for a landing. When Scott returned to Hut Point in January 1911, he found that a window had been forced open so that the hut was filled with snow. Scott assumed that Shackleton's party had done this to gain entry and had not bothered to repair it. He wrote angrily in his journal: 'Men who come to such places as this should leave what comfort they can to welcome those who follow.'

▲ In January 1909, Shackleton and his men got further South than any other explorers.

Shackleton's expedition was successful. By following the Beardmore **Glacier**, a route was found from the Great Ice Barrier to the South Polar plateau. However Shackleton had to turn back before reaching the South Pole, when his food began to run short.

New plans

Shackleton's expedition encouraged Scott to make definite plans for a new voyage to Antarctica. Although Scott had not approved of Shackleton, he did learn a great deal from his experiences. Like Shackleton, he decided to take **Siberian ponies** with him to McMurdo Sound.

Scott was determined to become the first person to reach the South Pole. In April 1909 the American explorer Robert E Peary claimed to be the first person in history to have reached the North Pole. Only the South Pole remained to be conquered. Scott made his aim very clear: 'The main object of this expedition is to reach the South Pole, and secure for the British Empire the honour of this achievement.'

▼ Shackleton's hut has been kept as a museum.

A new expedition

▲ Scott was bored with London society. He busied himself raising funds for his next trip.

Scott planned his new expedition as if it was a military exercise. He knew the expedition would take two or three years. The Antarctic climate meant that little could be done during the long, harsh southern winter. And the southern summers were all too short.

The first summer, from November 1910 to February 1911, would be taken up with sailing to the Antarctic, building a hut and setting up large stores of food and equipment along the route to the Pole.

The second summer, of 1911-12, would be taken up with the journey to the Pole and back. It had to be completed before the onset of winter.

Money and ships

First, Scott had to raise money to pay for the new expedition. He opened an office in London. Scott found it hard to raise the large amount of money he needed. The idea of Antarctic travel was no longer new, and Shackleton had only just come back to Britain.

Scott did his best. Week after week he toured Britain, giving lectures and appealing for money. Slowly the money came in. However it was only after he received a grant of £20 000 from the British government that his fortunes began to pick up.

Naturally enough, Scott wanted to use the *Discovery* again for the expedition. After all, it had been specially built for Antarctic waters and he knew it well. However the ship had been sold to new owners, the Hudson Bay Company. Scott was unable to persuade them to let him use it again. Instead, he had to buy the 57 metre (187 foot) long *Terra Nova*, a three-masted wooden ship with both engines and sails.

The team members

Scott now began to choose the team of experts who would come with him on the journey. His first choice was 'Bill' Wilson, a doctor and an artist who could make

▲ The *Terra Nova*

paintings of the expedition. 'Bill' Wilson was also a **zoologist**, a scientist who studies birds and animals. Wilson and Shackleton had gone with Scott on the long sledge run towards the South Pole in 1902.

Scott made Lieutenant Edward Evans his second-in-command. 'Teddy' Evans was to become a war hero in 1917, during the First World War. He eventually became an Admiral.

Captain Lawrence Oates, a young army officer, was an important member of the team. Captain Oates became Scott's expert on ponies. The other team members were

very fond of him and called him 'The Soldier'.

Two naval members of the 1901-04 team also joined the new expedition. Leading Stoker William Lashly and Petty Officer Edgar Evans had the skills, strength and courage that he needed.

Over 8000 men volunteered to come with Scott. From these he chose an expert on huskies called Cecil Meares and another doctor, Surgeon-Lieutenant Edward Atkinson. He also selected a Norwegian skier called Trygve Gran and a brilliant photographer called Herbert Ponting. Scientists who came on the expedition included weather experts and **geologists**, who wanted to study the rocks of the Antarctic.

▼ Some of Scott's team members. From left to right – Cherry-Garrard, Bowers, Oates, Meares and Atkinson.

Ponies, dogs and pemmican

▲ Scott testing motor sledges in Norway. They were to fail him during his bid to reach the South Pole.

Scott decided to take some huskies with him this time, despite his unfortunate experience on the last expedition. However he did not want to rely on them, and so he decided to look for other ways of moving food and equipment across the ice.

He went to Norway and was impressed by a new **motor sledge** which had just been invented. This type of sledge used **caterpillar tracks**, like those which were later used on the first tanks. These allowed the vehicle to crawl over slippery surfaces. He ordered three motor sledges for the expedition.

Scott's more traditional sledges were based on those used by Fridtjof Nansen when he explored the Arctic. They were lightweight and made of wood.

Siberian ponies of the kind used by Shackleton in 1907 could be bought in Russia. Nineteen were purchased, along with 34 huskies. These were to join the ship in New Zealand. Scott thought that the tough little ponies would be so used to living in the freezing climate of Siberia that they would be ideal working animals for the Antarctic.

Food and supplies

The team also put together the supplies and equipment they would need for the expedition. The food had to be easy to store and to carry.

▲ The Siberian ponies were cared for by Captain Lawrence Oates.

Scott ordered large quantities of **pemmican**. This food had been invented long before by the peoples of North America. When Native Americans went on long hunting expeditions they often dried meat, ground it into a paste and then made it into small cakes. In the Cree language, these were called *pimikan*. Early European settlers also tried chewing this food on long journeys.

Scott's team bought in supplies of biscuits, flour, oatmeal, chocolate and sugar. In those days, people knew less than we do today about food and energy. Today, explorers of very cold lands would take with them more fatty foods, such as butter, for energy. They would also take food with more **vitamin C**, for their health.

Food also had to be brought along for the animals, hay for the ponies and meat and biscuits for the dogs.

The food and other supplies were all very heavy to carry. It was agreed that the food would be placed in depots along the route to the South Pole. These dumps would be well marked with cairns and flags to make them easy to see. There was no fear of anyone stealing the food, of course, since no one lived in Antarctica. The wild animals and birds lived only on the coast and were never seen inland.

Keeping out the cold

The clothing used by Scott and his men was much the same as that used by the Inuit people of the Arctic. This type of clothing is still sometimes used in the Arctic today. That is why we use Inuit words such as *anorak* and *parka* to describe such garments. All the members of the expedition wore thick underclothing and woollen shirts.

At night in their tents they slept in sleeping bags made from reindeer skin.

▼ The kind of clothing worn by Scott and his team in the Antarctic.

Storms and fears

▲ Scott and his team having a meeting on board the *Terra Nova*

On 15 June 1910 the *Terra Nova* set sail from Cardiff, Wales, bound for distant Antarctica. The voyage was a long one. The ship called in at ports on the way, in South Africa, Australia and New Zealand. In foreign cities, Scott tried to raise more money for the expedition.

It was when he reached Melbourne in Australia that Scott received a piece of news that he found very disturbing. It was a cable from the Norwegian explorer, Roald Amundsen. The message was simple: '*BEG LEAVE TO INFORM YOU PROCEEDING ANTARCTICA*'. In other words, Scott and his team were not going to be on their own in Antarctica.

The Norwegian explorer had always wanted to be the first to reach the North Pole. However in 1909, after hearing the news about Robert Peary's success, he had changed his mind. He had decided to try for the South Pole instead.

Scott was annoyed. He realised with a sinking heart that, for all his efforts, he might yet lose the race to reach the South Pole. In those days, internationally organised expeditions were unknown. Each country competed with its neighbours for the honour and the glory.

Sailing south

Scott said farewell to his wife, Kathleen, in Dunedin, New Zealand, and set sail from nearby Port Chalmers on 20 November 1910. This was the port nearest to McMurdo Sound, where he had set up his base camp in 1901-04. The final leg of the voyage had begun.

The *Terra Nova* was heavily laden with stores, fuel and equipment. The ship soon sailed into severe storms in the southern oceans. About a third of the coal piled up on decks was washed overboard. A large amount of petrol for the motor sledges was also lost. The weather was so bad that even the dogs and ponies on board became sick.

▼ While the fine weather lasted, supplies were unloaded and piled up on the shore.

Landfall

On 4 January 1911, six weeks after leaving New Zealand, the members of the British Antarctic expedition landed on the shores of McMurdo Sound. It was the height of the short Antarctic summer. Scott wrote in his journal that he 'could almost imagine a warm summer day in England'. Only two weeks later a heavy snow fall reminded him that this was the Antarctic. The summer would soon be over.

The crew of the ship, and the 25 men who were going to spend the winter in the Antarctic, quickly set up camp. It took them just over a week to unload their stores. The ship was anchored about 2.5 km (1.5 miles) from the shore. They used a thick ice shelf as a **wharf** on which to unload equipment. Unluckily the warm weather made the ice melt. One of the three motor sledges was lost when it fell through the ice. It sank to the seabed.

▼ Once the team left the base hut they would camp in small tents. Here, Evans, Bowers, Wilson and Scott share a meal in their tent. Food was heavy to carry so it was carefully rationed. Inset is one day's supply for one man.

McMurdo Sound

▲ The members of the expedition had to live and work together as a team.

Instead of setting up their base at Hut Point, the team built a new hut at a place which Scott named Cape Evans. It was essential that the hut should be ready well before the start of the Antarctic winter.

For this reason the hut, which was made of timber, had been made in sections before the expedition left New Zealand. The hut was 16 metres (52 feet) long and 8 metres (26 feet) wide. The walls had two separate layers of boarding. Seaweed was stuffed in between to keep out the cold. The roof was also made of several layers of boarding and another layer of seaweed.

To the south and east of the hut the team members piled up the hay for the ponies. This would give extra protection against the bitter Antarctic winds. When the hut was ready for living in, less than a fortnight later, Scott was delighted: 'We are simply overwhelmed with its comfort', he wrote.

Getting down to work

All the team members had their jobs to do. The photographer built a **darkroom**

▼ The laboratory set up in the hut at Cape Evans

in part of the hut, so that he could develop his pictures. The scientists set up a tiny **laboratory**. Other parts of the hut were used to store books, scientific instruments and a record player.

Although Scott's main aim was to be the first person to reach the South Pole, he also knew that it was the work of the scientists which would provide the world with fresh and vital information about Antarctica.

An evening at Cape Evans base

The failing light and approach of supper drives us home again with good appetites about 5 or 6 o'clock. The cooks rival one another in preparing tasty dishes of fried seal liver. After supper we have an hour or so of smoking and conversation – a cheering, pleasant hour. Afterwards we tail off one by one, spread out our sleeping bags, take off our shoes and creep into comfort, for our reindeer bags are really warm and comfortable now. Thanks to the blubber lamps and to a fair supply of candles, we can read for another hour or two.

From the journal of Captain Scott

To the depot and back

Before winter started, team members hurried to take food, oil and equipment to a storage dump which they called One-Ton Depot. This was about 210 km (130 miles) from Cape Evans. Scott had wanted to set up the depot 48 km (30 miles)

nearer to the South Pole. Unluckily he was prevented by bad weather. This short distance was later to make all the difference between life and death.

Scott tried out both dogs and ponies during the depot runs. At first he thought that the ponies were going to be 'real good'. In the end, though, it was found that they did not like the Antarctic blizzards. The ponies often sank in soft snow, and by the end of the trip a number had died. The huskies were better suited to the ice and snow, but they were difficult to handle. At one point the huskies caught sight of a whale offshore, and tore after it, in the wrong direction.

▼ The menu of the Mid-winter's day celebration meal at the base camp

The journey overland

▲ Captain Scott worked in his small room through the long winter.

While expedition members worked on their scientific projects and set up the depot, the *Terra Nova* prepared to set sail for New Zealand. Before the ship left, it took a team of six men along the coast to explore further.

The *Terra Nova* returned with bad news for Captain Scott. Roald Amundsen's ship was anchored in the Bay of Whales. The Norwegian explorer had over 100 dogs and was 100 km (60 miles) nearer than Scott to the South Pole. Scott now realised that Amundsen, relying on dog teams rather than ponies, would be able to leave for the Pole much earlier than he would.

During the winter, Scott and his men did their best to while away the long dark hours. At last spring came and their spirits rose. The overland journey would soon begin, and with it the race to the Pole. Each day Scott sat in his tiny office in the hut, planning the details of the journey and writing up his journal.

Across the ice

On 1 November 1911 the British team at last set off into that vast expanse of ice and snow, the Great Ice Barrier. It was the

▲ Setting up a depot for later use

start of the Antarctic summer. Scott knew they had about three or four months at the most to get to the South Pole and then back again.

The whole expedition set off, divided into groups. Each had its special job to do. Teams of Siberian ponies and huskies pulled the sledges, which were laden high with oil for heating and lighting, equipment, and food for both humans and animals.

The two motor sledges had gone on ahead, but they soon proved unreliable. They broke down only 80 km (50 miles) from Cape Evans. Their loads now had to be hauled by the men.

As the expedition moved forward, food and supplies for use on the return journey were dropped off at a series of depots. The loads carried on the sledges got lighter day by day. Steadily, they made their way across the ice.

Delays and soft snow

As Scott had feared, the ponies had trouble when the ground was covered in deep, powdery snow. Further delays occurred at the start of December, when a blizzard blew for four days on end. The team members could not leave their tents and the biting cold weakened the ponies.

As they came to the mountains which bordered the high polar plateau, they began to run short of hay for the ponies. They had no choice. The weakest animals were shot first and the loads they carried were moved to other sledges. The pony meat was fed to the dogs. They also stored some of the meat at the depots, since the ice and snow would keep it fresh for use on the return journey. Two days later, Scott sent the dogs back to base, with some of the team members.

Dr Wilson and the other members of the team preferred to haul the sledges themselves rather than put up with ponies struggling in soft snow, with unruly dogs or unreliable motors.

▼ The huskies pulled sledges loaded with supplies.

A battle lost and won

▲ The team setting out across the ice sheet toward the polar plateau.

The British team was now near the Beardmore Glacier, the route discovered by Shackleton's expedition. There were twelve men left, with three sledges to haul up the slope by themselves. Each man was harnessed to a sledge using a wide canvas belt. This spread the weight of the sledge evenly across the body.

They were helped by the fact that the wooden sledges they were using had such lightweight frames. Even so, when laden with food and equipment for several weeks, each sledge weighed nearly half a tonne.

Most of the team wore skis, but they were not very expert at using them. They found the journey uphill exhausting. It took a long time to reach the top of the glacier. It was very steep and split by deep cracks, or **crevasses**.

There was still a long way to go to the South Pole when they were again delayed by bad weather. Although this was the Antarctic summer, the weather could be as cold as any winter in Europe.

By 20 December Scott had reached a point about 320 km (200 miles) from the

▼ While Scott's men were struggling up the Beardmore Glacier, Amundsen's team had arrived at the South Pole.

Pole. He decided to reduce his team further, sending back four men. They were very upset. Scott wrote in his journal: 'I have just told off the people to return tomorrow night. All are disappointed. I dreaded this necessity of choosing – nothing could be more heartrending.'

The unknown truth

As Scott wrote these words, he was unaware that he had already lost the race to the South Pole. Roald Amundsen and his men had already arrived there, raising the Norwegian flag at 3.00pm on 14 December 1911 – when the British were just beginning to struggle up the Beardmore Glacier.

Amundsen had first left his base at the Bay of Whales as early as 8 September, but had been forced back by severe weather. In the end, it was not until 20 October, just 11 days before Scott, that he had been able to set out.

Amundsen's team was made up of only five men, four sledges and 52 dogs. Wisely, the Norwegians had put their faith in huskies. After all, the Inuit used dogs to move across ice and snow in the Arctic. If dogs were good enough for them, then they were surely good enough for Antarctic explorers. The dogs pulled the sledges up on to the plateau by way of the Axel Heiberg Glacier.

The battle to reach the South Pole had been won. Amundsen's careful planning, and the physical fitness of his team, helped to make sure that his expedition was successful.

▼ Amundsen's team was lightly equipped, and travelled fast, using huskies to pull the sledges.

An awful place

▲ Camping in deep snow

As Roald Amundsen and his companions made their way back home, Captain Scott and the seven men left in his party pressed on towards the South Pole. By 4 January 1912 they were about 240 km (150 miles) from their goal. It would now only take a few days, but Scott still had to ask another three men to return to base. In his journal, Scott wrote: 'Teddy Evans is terribly disappointed but has taken it very well and behaved like a man. Poor old Crean wept and even Lashly was affected.' Evans later said, 'little did we think that we would be the last to see them alive.'

The returning party, led by 'Teddy' Evans, had a hair-raising journey back to base. They made fast time across the Polar plateau, as they fixed a sail onto the sledge to drive it along. They then took a short but scary route down the glacier, dodging deadly crevasses. By this time 'Teddy' Evans was ill with **scurvy**. Thomas Crean

▼ Scott and his team placed the Union Jack at the South Pole alongside the Norwegian flag placed there by Amundsen.

▲ Scott and his team beside Amundsen's tent at the South Pole

and William Lashly saved his life by getting him back to McMurdo Sound before the winter set in once more.

The moment of truth

In the meantime, Scott continued south. He had taken on Henry Bowers, one of Evans' sledge team, and so had an extra mouth to feed on rations planned for four. This also meant that there was an extra person in the already crowded tent. Bowers did not even have a pair of skis. He had to walk to the South Pole on foot.

It was Bowers who first spotted a black speck in the distance. It was on 16 January, and they were only about 32 km (20 miles) from the South Pole. With sinking hearts, the five men approached. They knew that in this white wilderness anything that was black must have been brought by humans. Sure enough, they found a flag, and: 'the remains of a camp and sledge tracks and ski tracks going and

coming and the clear trace of dog's paws – many dogs.' They knew now, for certain. They had lost the race.

Scott at the Pole

They carried on, until at last, on 18 January 1912, the British team stood at the South Pole itself. Captain Robert Scott, Dr 'Bill' Wilson, Lieutenant Henry Bowers, Captain Lawrence Oates and Petty Officer Edgar Evans stared around them at the endless snowy waste.

At the Pole they found the Norwegian tent and a letter written by Roald Amundsen. The explorer asked Scott to forward it to King Haakon VII of Norway, in case he and his men failed to return home.

'Great God, this is an awful place!' Scott wrote in his diary. Then he added, almost in despair: 'Now for the run home and a desperate struggle. I wonder if we can do it?'

God help us!

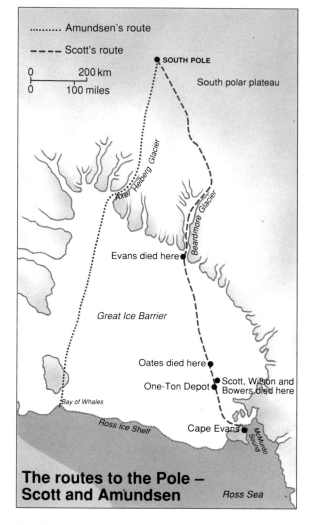

The routes to the Pole – Scott and Amundsen

.... Amundsen's route

- - - - Scott's route

SOUTH POLE

South polar plateau

South pole plateau

Axel Heiberg Glacier

Beardmore Glacier

Evans died here

Great Ice Barrier

Oates died here

One-Ton Depot

Scott, Wilson and Bowers died here

Bay of Whales

Ross Ice Shelf

Cape Evans

McMurdo Sound

Ross Sea

The biting chill seemed far worse because of the high winds and the occasional blizzard. On 24 January, Scott wrote that 'things were beginning to look a little serious'. He was worried because Lawrence Oates and Edgar Evans were already suffering from **frostbite**, yet they still had a huge distance to go.

All felt tired. Because their progress was slower than expected, their food was not enough to last them from one depot to the next. When blizzards delayed them, they had to reduce the amount they ate. Soon they were desperately hungry.

Disaster on the glacier

As Scott's team clambered down the Beardmore Glacier, Petty Officer Evans had

▼ Conditions inside the team tent were very cramped.

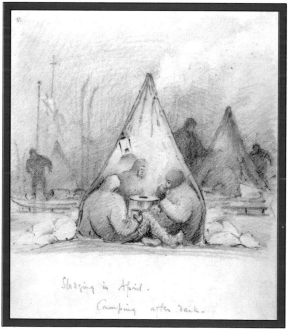

On the outward journey, the dream of reaching the South Pole had kept Scott and his men going. Now all they had ahead of them was 1300 km (800 miles) of 'solid dragging – and goodbye to most of the day-dreams'. The heavy strain of pulling the sledges was soon to affect them all.

To make matters worse, the weather was bitterly cold – as low as minus 30°C (minus 22°F) at the South Pole, even though this was the Antarctic summer.

▲ A painting of Oates going out into the blizzard

a fall. It may have damaged his brain. On 6 February, Scott wrote that Evans was 'the chief anxiety now'. Again, on 14 February: 'Evans is giving us serious anxiety.' On 16 February, Evans stopped the march 'on some trivial excuse'. But in fact, he was dying. Scott described the next day as 'very terrible'. Evans had fallen unconscious and died in the night.

The four men remaining still had 640 km (400 miles) to go. When they finally left the glacier they were at least able to eat fresh meat again, after reaching a depot left on the outward journey. They all voted the meal on 19 February, 'a sort of stew', the best 'they had ever had on a sledge journey.'

Ten days later the weather was 'desperately cold'. The night time temperature had fallen to minus 40°C (minus 40°F). On 4 March Scott wrote: 'Things look very black indeed', and on the next day his words were: 'One can only say "God help us!".'

Into the darkness

One reason that they were making such slow progress was that Captain Lawrence Oates was holding them back. He had been very badly affected by frostbite and found it very painful to walk. On 11 March, Scott noted that 'Oates is very near the end'.

Oates knew he was holding up the rest of the party. The other three had no chance of returning in safety so long as he was there to hold them back. On 16 March 1912, in an heroic act, Lawrence Oates left the tent and went out into the howling blizzard, knowing that he would never return. He told the others, 'I am just going outside and may be sometime.'

Scott, Wilson and Bowers knew, of course, that Oates was going out to die for their sake. Scott wrote: 'though we tried to dissuade him, we knew it was the act of a brave man and an English gentleman. We all hope to meet the end with a similar spirit.'

In memory

Scott and his companions were now in no doubt that the end was near. They had hoped to meet up with a team from Cape Evans. In fact, Cherry-Garrard waited at One-Ton Depot, only 112 km (70 miles) away, until 10 March. Then, appalling weather and a shortage of dog food forced him to return to base.

Scott, Wilson and Bowers kept on going for two or three more days. On Wednesday 21 March, Scott wrote: 'Got within 11 miles of depot Monday; had to lay up all yesterday in severe blizzard.' They were so near and yet so far. As ill luck would have it, the blizzard raged all week. On Thursday 29 March they were still there and still alive, but had had no food or hot drink for a day. Scott wrote

▲ The final entry in Scott's journal

the final entry in his journal that day: 'We shall stick it out to the end, but we are getting weaker, of course, and the end cannot be far. It seems a pity, but I do not think I can write more. For God's sake

▼ Scott's base camp hut today

look after our people.' Their frozen bodies were discovered at the start of the next Antarctic summer.

London mourns

The news from Antarctica shocked the people of Britain. Scott and his team were hailed as national heroes. A memorial service was held in St Paul's Cathedral in London, attended by King George V and 8000 people. Scott's widow, Kathleen, and the wives of his companions, were paid special pensions by the British government, and given money raised by a public appeal.

Some people criticised Scott. They said he should have paid more attention to the food his party had to eat. One illness from which they suffered, scurvy, is caused by lack of vitamin C. Scott failed to train his team as skiers, and made a mistake when he took five men instead of four on the final push to the Pole. Some said he wasted time collecting rock samples. Most people agreed that, like the Norwegians, he should have relied on dog teams rather than ponies or motor sledges.

However no one doubted the bravery of Scott and his team, and this has never been forgotten.

The last wilderness

Robert Scott's expedition was followed by many others. On 29 November 1929 the American pilot Richard Byrd became the first person in history to fly to the South Pole. In 1946 Byrd led an American expedition of 4700 men in 13 ships to map a large section of Antarctica.

Ten years later a British Commonwealth expedition led by Vivien Fuchs crossed the continent for the first time. They travelled from Shackleton Base on the Weddell Sea to Scott Base in Victoria Land, via the South Pole. Fuchs took geological readings on the way. By this time the United States and the Soviet Union had set up permanent bases in Antarctica, with groups of scientists living there all year round.

We know now that the frozen wastes of Antarctica cover rich **mineral deposits.** Some people would like to see these mined and used. Other people believe that the Antarctic should become an international park, undisturbed and unpopulated except by wildlife and scientists. Perhaps the continuing peace of this vast wilderness would be a fitting memorial to Scott and his companions.

▼ The McMurdo Station (US) houses over 900 people in summer.

Glossary

base camp: the chief camp of an expedition, used for organising and supply

blizzard: a snowstorm in a strong wind. Snow or powdered ice driven by the wind makes it hard to see

cable: to send a telegram, by means of an electric wire or cable

cairn: a pile of stones erected to mark a route or a special place, such as a depot or a grave. Antarctic explorers used blocks of ice to make cairns

caterpillar tracks: metal plates linked around driving wheels, as on a modern tank or digger. They allow a vehicle to travel over mud or snow

continent: one of the world's chief land masses, such as Africa or Asia

crevasses: deep cracks in the surface of a glacier

darkroom: the room used by a photographer to develop and print photographs

depot: a store of food or equipment, set aside for use at a future date

frostbite: a serious injury caused to flesh when it is exposed to severe cold. Fingers, toes or noses may become blistered and badly damaged

gale force: a wind speed of about 62-74 kph (39-46 mph). Winds above gale force are classed as strong gales, storms, violent storms and hurricanes

geologist: a scientist who studies rocks and the structure of the Earth

glacier: a great river of ice which moves very slowly, scraping away the rock along its course

husky: a breed of working dog, originally from the Arctic. Huskies are mainly used to pull sledges across snow and ice

ice sheet: a thick layer of snow which over many years has piled up and turned into ice.

ice shelf: steep cliffs formed where an ice sheet melts or meets the sea

iceberg: a great block of ice which has broken off an ice sheet or a glacier to float in the sea

journal: a day-by-day diary or record of events

laboratory: a place where a scientist carries out experiments or examines specimens

marooned: stranded, unable to sail. In polar regions, ships may become trapped in the ice

mineral deposits: rocks or soil containing metals, coal or oil which may be extracted by mining or drilling

motor sledge: a sledge fitted with a petrol engine which drives caterpillar tracks, like those on a digger. The tracks enable it to move backwards or forwards

navigator: a person who steers a course by air or sea

pemmican: a Native American dish of dried meat. Both Scott and Amundsen ate it in Antarctica

Pole Party: the members of Scott's expedition who were selected to go to the South Pole

plateau: a large flat-topped mountain or upland area

research station: a place where scientists carry out experiments, take readings and compile records

scurvy: a dangerous disease caused by a lack of fresh fruit or vegetables, which contain vitamin C

Siberian ponies: thick-coated ponies first bred in Siberia, the coldest part of Russia

specimens: samples of plants, animals or rocks taken for scientific study

vitamin C: goodness found in fresh fruit and vegetables, which keeps us healthy

wharf: a level area or quay used to load and unload ships

wireless sets: radio, or 'wireless telegraphy', had only recently been invented in the 1900s. Explorers such as Scott and Amundsen still had to travel without any radio contact with the outside world

zoologist: a scientist who studies animal life

Further Reading

The Expeditions of Amundsen, by Richard Humble (Franklin Watts, 1991)

Exploring the Poles, by Derek Cullen and John Murray-Robertson (Macmillan Education, 1987)

Let's go to Antarctica, by Keith Lye (Franklin Watts, 1984)

New Frontiers: Exploration in the Twentieth Century: The Arctic and Antarctic, by Cass R Sandak (Franklin Watts, 1987)

The Race to the South Pole, by Rupert Matthews (Wayland, 1990)

Index